The Boss From Hell

Gale Jackson

Gale@GaleWindsCreations.com

Editor & Coach
Chas Ridley

Artist, Cover Co-Designer
Denise Jackson

Technical Assistance
Lauren Creech

Published by Gale Jackson 2017

The Boss From Hell

Gale Jackson, Publisher

Gale@GaleWindsCreations.com

Contents

Acknowledgements

Thank you to all who took the time to listen, encourage, and build me up. This book would not have been possible without your support.

My dear daughter Denise, thank you for taking excellent care of me and welcoming me into your beautiful home, without pressure, while I wrote this book.

My son Tramell, thank you for reading my first draft. I appreciate your honesty and candor. I was pleased to hear that you liked the book and thought it was hilarious.

Thank you my son, son-in-law and daughter for believing in your mom. I love you.'

Thanks also to the love of my life. You showed great patience with me when I had to quit a job or two due to a boss from hell. Thank you for standing by me.

My sisters and brothers – through blood relationships and through heart-felt selection, you listened to me about my bosses, work, and many other things in life. I love each and every one of you.

My dear friends, many of you are like family to me. I love and thank you for your love and confidence in me. May God continue to bless you.

A special thank-you to Onyx, grand-dog, for your unconditional love and affection through some stressful, sad days.

Chapter 1
The Workplaces

Bosses From Hell

I would like to send a shout-out to each ex-boss from hell who made significant contributions to past and present employees. Thank you, Boss, for our sleepless nights, unwanted weight gain or loss, high blood pressure, broken relationships, premature thinning and excessive early graying of our hair. Last, but not least, thank you for the raging flame that reared its ugly head inside me more times than I felt comfortable with – a feeling I never knew existed until I worked for you. I tell you, you can break the strongest man or woman down. My sincere prayer is that I never work for you or anyone like you again. Amen.

All disturbing feelings aside, I thank you for unexpected growth If I had not worked for you, I might never have discovered this part of my divine calling, which includes writing this book, *The Boss From Hell*.

Motivational Bosses

You are truly a blessing. Thank you for adding value to the lives of those of us who have had the honor and privilege of working under your professional leadership. You are an excellent mentor. You make the world a brighter place to work, and you set a positive example of what great leadership is all about. Working for you was a pleasure. You rock!

Co-Workers

I would like to extend another shout-out to many of my former co-workers. You know exactly what I am talking about, because you have been subjected to the same foolish, tiring games and crazy treatment from the boss from hell.

I love each one of you. We pulled each other through those dark days when it was like a battlefield at work. As we used to sing, "Don't push me, 'cause I'm close to the edge, I'm trying not to lose my head, ha-ha. It's like a jungle sometimes, it makes me wonder how I keep from goin' under, ha-ha." A shout-out, also, to Grandmaster Flash for the song "The Message" that gave us those words that became our theme song.

We kept each other laughing when we were not crying or consoling one another. You are all rock stars. Don't let anyone tell you anything different. Miss you much.

Chapter 2

The Interview

Let the acting begin, cameras roll, and now take the front of the stage (Act 1). You know how we do it. In preparation for the interview, you get your best suit cleaned or purchase a new one. You shine your shoes, make sure your hair or bald head is looking fabulous. In other words, do whatever it takes to look smashing, Darling, cool, fine, all the way live. Phatt, chronk, classy, professional, or whatever you call it to feel you've got it going on.

On the day of the interview, after you are dressed and before you walk out the door, you do what I call a motivational prep/self-love talk. Look at yourself in the mirror, wink your right eye, blow a kiss at your dressed-up self, and then say, "Wow! Wow! I look good! I really look good. I would hire me. I've got this. Yeah, I've definitely got this." And off you go praying for positive results and divine direction.

I won't insult your intelligence by explaining the reason for an interview. We all know the interview process is meant to determine whether your skill-set matches what the potential employer is looking for, and whether the company and position are a good fit for what you are looking for.

Always keep in mind that you are interviewing the company even as they are interviewing you. Sometimes we are at a point in our lives where we need a job. Or we just need what looks like an opportunity to prove ourselves and get paid.

The Interviewer and the Clue

Interviewers each have different styles of interviewing. As a job-seeker, we never know what we are going to get until we are actually in the interview. The sharp interviewee realizes that the interviewer is looking for reasons to either eliminate or hire you.

In today's job market, many interviews start with a telephone screen, then progress to the next level, with the final interview being the first face-to-face meeting.

I have a serious question for each of you. Have you ever blamed yourself for not getting at least one clue of what you were getting yourself into? Or have you had a deep, penetrating bad feeling about someone or something and just shaken it off or ignored it?

Well, my friend, let me tell you about one of my interviews.

I was relocating to another state, and a recruiter called me regarding a position with his company. Mike was as delightful and pleasant as could be and, at the time when I spoke with him, he gave me the impression I would be reporting to him. We had a great interview, and I was very excited about meeting with Mike and the possibility of working with this great boss.

Mike told me that the next step was to meet with one of the directors from the corporate office. I agreed to meet, and another telephone screening was set up for me. The interview went great. Peggy had a different style – not as friendly as Mike, but nevertheless she was informative, engaging and professional.

I talked with a relative after interviewing with Mike and Peggy, and she could hear the excitement in my voice about this position.

Soon I was told that the next step would be to meet the Regional Director. Again, we "met" on a telephone interview. I have to say Linda was interesting. She had a contagious but annoyingly loud laugh, and I know that it takes all types of personalities. Well, this woman took me from point A to point B at the speed of a rocket. She worked me over big time. She asked me to jump, and I said "How high?" and I made it through one challenge after another. She then told me that she was sending me a personality profile, and asked me why I wanted to work for her.

I started to say, "Lady! I don't want to work for you," but I reframed and thought a bit. You see, I needed a job.

When I finally gave her my answer of why I wanted to work for her and this company, it was not good enough for her. She told me to send her an email on why she should hire me and the reason I felt I would like to work for her. At that point, I started to say, "Let's just forget this," but then I thought about how much I really enjoyed talking with Mike and Peggy.

Plus the position did sound like a great career opportunity.

I must admit the woman was good at her job. She had worked in direct hire staffing for more than 20 years, and she made tons of money from it.

At last, the interview was over. When the same relative who had seen me after the first two interviews with that company arrived home that evening, she looked very puzzled. Patty stared at me and said, "You look like you have been through the wringer. What happened to you? You have veins popping out on the sides of your temples and your eyes look red and swollen."

This should have been a big clue. Who could do this much damage on a telephone interview? Again, I ask you, who could do this much damage on a phone interview? Bingo! You've got it! A boss from hell.

I was questioned again by the same family member. "Are you sure you want to work for this company? I was too worn out even to comment.

You would think I'd have had sense enough to get the clue. "No, not I," said the foolish one. I ignored it all. I just thought I was losing my touch. I had not looked for a job in about four years, so I must be rusty with interviewing. I reasoned with myself and made many excuses for me and for her. Trust me, I had lingering doubts for hours after interviewing with this lady.

Even though I had never before in my life been told I looked that bad after an interview, I can now tell you that I never worked for a chick like this one, either, in my 20-plus years in the workforce. She was "too much chili for this hot dog." I will elaborate on Sybil at another time. Yes, Sybil. My very dear friend Lee Coleman gave her this name. Lee renamed several of my other past bosses also. She, along with many others, has had the misfortune of listening to many stories about my bosses from hell.

Chapter 3

After the Interview,

the Real Deal

Deal or no deal? Okay, there was no banker involved in this transaction. This is the real deal, holyfield. Work-related, of course. The interview is over and you are just settling into your new position. You have not even been working on your new job for a month, and you already know the answer to: "What did I get myself into?"

Things are changing around you faster than a sinking boat. You are gasping for air and suffocating every day. Okay, I will say it. You know you have made another mistake. You thought this was the one – and you thought wrong. You start asking yourself, "Shall I stay or shall I go?" In less than two weeks!

Many times you start to think or feel inside that this place is weird or strange. But you always say to yourself that this is a job, many people in the world do not have a job, and okay, you know this sounds like Mom when she was trying to talk you into eating something you did not like as a child. Yes, you remember those words: "Eat it. Some people in this world don't have food. Children are starving in China." Thanks, Mom. It did not work then, and it won't work now. So brace yourself for the long ride, partner.

Admit it! You know already that you have to make another change. You don't know when, but you have to acknowledge that another move is on the horizon. And you do not feel good about this.

You quietly say to yourself, "Management, management, management." It is a well-known fact that most people leave their jobs due to poor management, not because of the company. Management has run many good employees off, running as though they were getting away from a bad nightmare. We will return to this subject later.

Chapter 4

The Boss From Hell's Games

I could tell you story after story, and still have many stories left to tell. I am sure that you, too, have either experienced or observed a boss from hell in action. In case you have not, let me tell you about a couple of bosses who inspired me to write this book.

Keep in mind that there is a difference between a boss who drives you crazy and a boss from hell. Please allow me the privilege of expounding on this matter.

Bosses who drive you crazy are difficult, and they sometimes make your life a working hell. But did you notice that I said "sometimes"? Every boss has some bad days, and with life's turns of events coupled with pressure at work, the average boss can occasionally snap. This boss that drives you crazy does not usually interrupt your job productivity.

On the other hand, it appears to me that the boss from hell is on a definite mission to interfere with your work productivity and then question why you do not have more to show for your time spent at work. You see, the boss from hell truly believes that she or he is adding to your professional success. Bosses from hell also like to fix things that are not broken. In fact, they spend countless hours belaboring over fixing things that are not broken or wasting the employees' time and the company's money.

You cannot convince these fireball rollers that you do not need their assistance, at least not in that area. They seem to have an inborn habit of pushing to assist you in the areas where you do not need help. They strongly feel that they are the best at moving their employees toward a company's goal while in truth they are going nowhere.

The meetings – don't get me started. The crazy boss has crazy meetings. But the boss from hell has ten meetings a week about the same matter, and sometimes has the same meetings for weeks or months on the same subject, while covering nothing.

I think you get the point. The crazy boss gets under your skin often; the boss from hell gets in your soul most of the time. You think of this boss day and night. The boss from hell has complete control over your thought process more hours than necessary.

You are living in a state of shock or bewilderment, attempting to understand what happened at work that day, and why it took place. But you never seem to understand, no matter how long you ponder. Okay! You have dreams about this boss, or should I say nightmares.

I mentioned Sybil in an earlier chapter. Sybil was a high-profile boss, traveling from state to state for the company. She was hiring, training, and motivating her staff, or so she thought. This lady had an infectious laugh and was very free-hearted. She would give you the shirt off her back (or the blouse). Yes, she was very giving in monetary ways. For example, she would often buy lunch for the month for the whole office. She not only bought lunch, but she put thought into every employee's preferences.

She could have you laughing one moment and crying the next second. In an hour or so, you were ready to pimp-slap her. She would build you up to tear you down. What a lady. Sybil was as different and as changing as her name indicates. Yes! In my humble opinion, she had a few different personalities. She was also very controlling. She made sure everyone understood exactly who was in charge. If she detected an inkling of self-confidence in an employee, she looked for ways to destroy it.

On a bad day or during a bad moment, Sybil would attempt to destroy the most hard-working and respectful manager in front of their team. She needed everyone to know that this manager was in place only because she, Sybil, allowed them to be in that position.

The next moment she could be laughing loud and uncontrollably, and pleasant. This was a constant roller-coaster ride without the excitement and pleasures of a true, natural and clean high.

Please don't get this twisted. I do not enjoy talking about the bosses from hell. In fact, I enjoy talking about the bosses from hell much less than they enjoy destroying the people who report to them.

Enough about Sybil Let's talk about another boss from hell.

Lady Love worked my nerves royally. She not only worked my nerves, but she worked everyone in the room, even the other bosses with the same-clout status. These good leaders were all amazed by her, but not in a good way. We will meet up again with Lady Love in the chapter on team-building. For now, though, let me start with how controlling she was. She enjoyed hearing herself talk. Mind you, no-one else wanted to hear what she had to say, but that didn't slow her down.

Lady Love should have been a drill sergeant or an ordering master. She occupied about 60 percent of your time during the day, and worked on taking up your evening when she could. She was a networking queen who only attended the networking events that were good for her schedule. You'd better believe, though, that her team was commanded to attend – last-minute or not.

Like Sybil, Lady Love enjoyed bringing her staff down to a humble state. If one of her employees acted like they thought they were great at anything, she made sure that they would re-think their position or question the skills they had been confident about. She took up most of the team's time, leading them into nowhere.

Let's add a little retail business here. Let's talk about Lady Z. In this case, "Z" stands for zealous In fact it stands for very zealous. Lady Z was so zealous that she ran over the majority of the people who reported to her, reducing her employees often to sadness, fears, and tears. She was a terrorizing young chick. She was insulting and demeaning, calculating and cold. She said one thing and did another, told you to do something and changed it without letting you know it was changed. Or she'd forget altogether that she had changed things, while accusing her staff of not getting it right.

As I have stated before, a boss from hell interferes with production. Lady Z is infamous for interfering with production. She hires people for her management team who have no talent and then questions the managers about why their staff are not succeeding. Somewhere down the road, you as a manager have to let those same people go. What a ball of confusion. And what a waste of the company's money.

On the surface, Lady Z appeared to be normal, a regular type of boss. At a glance, you would believe she was helpful, kind and on your side, at least at the beginning of the boss-employee relationship. In fact, though, she made everyone's job harder than it had to be.

I could have called her Lady C, where the "C" stands for Control Freak. Yes, Lady Z was a controlling maniac. As an example, while working for her, you had no days off. You might have days off scheduled, and might even be so foolish as to make plans for rest or something pleasant with your family on those days. Rethink it! I have watched Lady Z call my friend on an off day after my friend had worked for 20 hours straight on window changes and floor moves, only to see my friend reduced to tears. Lady Z is known for focusing on the one small thing that was not 100% perfect instead of looking at the large things that were 200% excellent.

This high-roller class act works for one of the most glamorous, impressive and prestigious companies in the world. The company is known for the high demands it places on its entire staff, from managers to co-managers and associates. They are the "Best of the Best." What I am saying here is that you have to be good in the first place for this company to keep you, and you surely would not last two to six years at a professional sweat shop like this one.

When Lady Z conducted her routine visits, the store manager always had a bigger job to do after the famous Lady Z left than before she came into the store. That bigger job would include building the co-managers' self-esteem back up and talking the rest of the loyal and good team members out of quitting. Last, but not least, was rebuilding the team's morale and her own self-respect as a manager after being blatantly berated and disrespected by her superior in front of all the staff.

Under the leadership of Lady Z, you could be pronounced a Golden Child today and then, in less than 24 hours, be treated like trash. Sounds like a boss from hell to me.

Chapter 5
Tip-Toeing on a Tulip

Tip-toeing on a tulip" is kind of like the expression "walking on eggshells." This is not an easy thing to do. When walking on eggshells, even if you walk lightly, you will still feel an uncomfortable sensation.

Tip-toeing on a tulip is mastering the same art, but without obvious discomfort. In other words, you have to step out of yourself and take on a different, near-to-impossible demeanor. Total transformation, a true out-of-body experience. You have to walk even lighter, faster, softer, all at once, not an easy task Okay, I made that expression up, and it fits the situations.

I can clearly remember one set of circumstances from a law firm. One of the associate attorneys was forced to tip-toe on a tulip or walk on eggshells most of his career with this law firm. This was a well-respected mid-size law firm in Texas. It was an excellent firm to work for – unless you worked for the boss from hell.

The boss from hell in this case was a litigation attorney, a rain-maker for the firm. We'll call him Mr. H He walked with a swagger that captivated his audience. He walked around the law firm as if he were James Bond or the Pink Panther. Yes, he was out of control. He truly believed that he was a god or a king, and that all around him must serve him.

This was one of my first experiences, a clear observation of a true boss from hell. He was arrogant, demanding, mean and commanding. Grown men jumped and moved quickly as he entered a room. He had a lasting effect on everyone he chose to speak to or work with.

He was another boss who did not give anyone else time to be productive. In fact, he interfered with work productivity in a major way. It was all about him.

Mind you, he was wise enough to be nice and professional with his clients, to maintain his rain-maker status. But for his employees, LOOK OUT!

I remember this man as though I'd seen him yesterday. I felt pain and hurt in the core of my soul for the associate who worked for Mr. H. Here was a very smart and hard-working attorney, but he was running around jumping to Mr. H's commands like a chicken with its head cut off. Yes, I could feel this man's pain.

This associate knew how to tip-toe on a tulip and look totally professional while doing so. He worked and worked with Mr. H, and displayed the patience of Job. All the while, he was being abused and misused.

Mr. H treated this young attorney like he was the most ignorant person he had ever beheld in his life. This was publicly expressed in front of the entire law firm.

This young associate was well-respected by the law firm, and by the entire group of partners (except Mr. H) as an excellent associate from a top-tier law school. But Mr. H would tell this attorney to research something for him, and in five minutes he would be paging him and yelling, "Where is the SOB?"

I don't know how the associate took it He must have been a saint. I thought I had a pretty even temper and spiritual grip in my life at the time. But I remember thinking to myself that, if Mr. H acted like that with me, I would have wanted to slap the shit out of him. I know that is wrong but, as you can see, a boss from hell upsets everyone around him, not just those who work directly for him. I can't feel comfortable working around a boss from hell, even though I've done it too many times."

Let's take this a little deeper. That particular associate came to the firm with thick black hair and, in two years, the young attorney was 65 percent gray. Yes, you are correct. I said "young man." Please keep in mind that I also had a ring-side observation of seeing this good family man cry. Yes, I said cry.

This all took place years ago, and I can still see the young attorney's face. He was a great guy. He was doing his job, making a living to support his family. His one problem was that he happened to report to a boss from hell.

I often wonder what makes a person tick who can treat a responsible adult like a child. Is it in the DNA? Or is it in the twisted mind? Or possibly the cold heart of such a person? I rest my case.

Chapter 6

Frozen

My definition/explanation of frozen – in reference to this book, *The Boss From Hell,* is a solid form that is as if it is non-existent, fear that locks you into a moment of silence, mental shock or a still surprise, temporary loss of free-range movement, lack of productivity. You cannot think or speak clearly when questioned by your boss. I could go on and on, but I believe you understand the point I am making.

I had sleepless nights and constant thoughts of work. I was shocked, sad, and concerned for myself and my co-workers. I was uncomfortable seeing grown people stripped of their confidence, something that had taken years for them to build, either through higher education, work experience, self-education, self-motivation, and/or other sources. I felt frozen on a job that was destroying my very being.

I could feel that the job had already destroyed a great deal in my co-workers. How in the world did we stay? How did we remain in such a place? Why are you still there? Are YOU frozen?

I vividly remember one incident with a very capable worker. She did the job of two people. She was fast, excited and eager to learn her new position, and she was darned good at it within a very short time. She would stay late, come in early, and work hard all day long. Her goal was to be the best in the business – in the legal staffing industry.

Lady Love and I had industry experience, but that woman in some areas could run circles around us, as I often mentioned to my boss. The Golden Child had the pure drive to succeed and the will to sustain that mindset.

I am not saying that Lady Love and I were not good at our jobs. We both came highly recommended by many experts in the field, and we have achieved levels of success. I will tell you in a bit why I named this boss Lady Love.

My point is that I watched that Golden Child go from upbeat to broken, from happy to sad, and from youthful to aged. She started experiencing shooting pain in her left arm and some temporary paralysis in the same area. This was one of the last straws for me, because I truly believe the Golden Child's body was beginning to react to the stress of being frozen in the work-place with its toxic environment.

It was hard for her to concentrate. I could feel the solid wall that would come up when Lady Love would put her down The Golden Child could not do anything right, according to Lady Love. This boss from hell declared anything and everything the Golden Child did unacceptable.

I often questioned what nut trained Lady Love in her ways? I strongly believe that many times we mimic what we have seen or how we have been treated in the past. People have told me long stories of how they were mistreated by mother, father, husband or ex-boss. Those people often had tears in their eyes when talking about the horrible mistreatment they had encountered. As I said earlier, these people had a variety of incidents. I felt very bad for many, and I identified with some.

What I cannot understand is what I saw down the road, when these people showed the same negative actions to others that they had so painfully spoken with me about. I am not trained to properly explain why I saw what I saw, but it did not look or feel normal to me. Also, it was inconsistent with what they had said to me as to who they really were, and how their experiences had made them better people.

I was puzzled, and I am still puzzled when people who spoke with me confidentially about times when they were poorly treated would later mistreat others in much the same way. I saw examples of this over and over. What a shock. Even more, what an education!

I strongly believe that we do not have to do the same bad things to others that happened to us. This is truly what I believe. I have worked very hard to not allow my own bad experiences to take a negative control of the rest of my life. For the life of me, I cannot understand why anyone would want to treat someone else as poorly as we/they have been treated in the past. It is just insane to me.

I have seen people frozen in an unhappy marriage. I have been frozen in a rough childhood situation and have viewed many others in the same situation. Perhaps you can explain to me, and please break it down for me, WHY any person would treat another person negatively in a way they had been mistreated and berated in the past.

It is getting cold in here. Let's just UN-FREEZE it.

Chapter 7

Team-Building

It amazes me how people who have no concept of team-building so often say things like, "Let's be a team." If you are anything like me, you are irritated by those words, especially from someone you know has not the slightest clue what the word TEAM means.

Usually this person is the one who is sabotaging the team spirit. I believe that a boss who does that likes hearing themselves talk or likes the sound of the word "team" without its real meaning. Perhaps mentioning "team-building" makes them feel they are great leaders or the directors of the team relationship.

I have gone over and over this subject, and still I cannot understand how these bosses think on the subject of teamwork Perhaps one of you will be able to break this down for me sometime. I need help here.

Perhaps, though, there is no way to understand how a boss who is conflicting, competitive and berating with a team they are supposed to lead could truly believe they are inspiring. Or that they are even connecting on any meaningful level with the people on their so-called team.

Members of one group I worked with often took long, puzzled looks at each other every time our boss would use the word "team." This was Lady Love, who you may remember from an earlier chapter. Everything was all about her. I must give it to the chick — she loved herself. She spent more time being proud of herself than actually working for the company. She truly was a team all by herself, a select VIP member promoting herself first, last and in between. What a team spirit she had. You go, girl!

Lady Love spent hours asking me questions about why our group was not a team. Or whether I thought we were a team. She was smart enough to notice that the team was jelling with each other even though not with her. She did not, however, see that, due to her attitude, nobody had the desire to connect with her.

I am a direct type of person, but even I could not say to her, "We are not a team because you are a crazy nut! You are full of yourself. Why don't you take a long look in the mirror at yourself? And then come back to ask me this foolish question again."

I still get a light headache when I think about all the ways we were not a team. I realized early in the game that we would not be very successful at building or branding the name of the company without a cohesive team. I tried explaining this to Lady Love until I was blue in the face, but she just did not get it, so I decided to rest my case on that subject.

Chapter 8

The Talk

This is the last chapter I completed. That should tell you a little something about how difficult this subject was for me to address.

I am sitting here with my left hand on my cheek and my other hand leaning on the table – stretched out with a slightly clenched fist. I am making myself nervous. My head is shaking from side to side, and no-one is here to witness my reactions except Onyx, my grand-dog. I am not doing this for show. It's difficult for me to think about the talk, because I feel my words so often fell on deaf ears.

How do I say this? There were so many talks and walks of "thank you for sharing your wisdom and being up-front about your feelings."

Have you ever tried to work things out with a boyfriend, girlfriend, husband, wife, other family member, or friend? Be honest. Things changed for one or two days, maybe even two weeks, right? But you did not give up. You did it again and again, until you could not take any more.

You said it this way and that way, over and over again. You gathered your thoughts, took a break, and started the process again. This time you hoped to get it right, to say it in the way that would finally work. Your goal was to get results and/or to let the other person know how they were affecting you and others, correct?

Yes, I honestly tried to be up-front with at least two of my bosses from hell. Each time I knew I was taking a chance. Still, I decided to have some dialogue about my feelings. Here are the short versions.

I called Sybil early in the morning from a conference room so I'd have privacy. I had thought about what to say to this boss from hell.

I started with some positive statements about working for her. She did, after all, know her stuff. She just had a problem directing others in a way that had a positive impact on their professional lives and comfort zones.

Sybil listened to me, and seemed okay with me addressing my concerns in this respectful manner, while still being up-front with her about the issues.

I said, "I really am seriously working hard and attempting to please you because it is important to me to succeed in the direct hire staffing business for me and for you." I also stated that I was appreciative of the fact she hired me and that she was confident I could do the job she hired me for, that I was part of what she felt was her dream team, which was a high compliment, an honor.

I then dropped a verbal bomb on her by mentioning that I was stressed out by her management style. She seemed surprised, and became totally silent.

I went deeper into my discussion. I felt much better after speaking with Sybil, and the conversation ended on a positive note. I was later told by a co-worker who had some clout that many recruiters had quit that job because they could not stand up to Sybil and let her know that she was driving them crazy.

I left the company a few weeks after my talk with Sybil, as I received an offer I could not refuse, with a significant pay increase. Picture me saying, "Color me gone!

With Lady Love, I talked, talked, and talked again and again, to no avail. She seemed to listen to what I had to say, and she thanked me for talking to her. However, she was so bent on her pride and determined to control everything and everyone that she just could not make a change. Not even if she thought you were right. Her excuse was that she had been too nice to the last people she managed and they took advantage of her.

I got it: someone else did the crime, and we got to do the time. Does this make any sense to you?

I have decided to devote more time to this subject in my future seminars and speaking engagements. I promise more juicy details there. The discussion will be aimed at protecting the innocent and assisting good managers with avoiding unethical actions in their management styles.

Chapter 9
The Walk

We have all heard Paul Simon's song, "50 Ways to Leave Your Lover" (Copyright © 1975 by Paul Simon Music). His advice is perfect for leaving a boss from hell, too. A thankful shout-out to Paul for these inspiring words: "You just slip out the back, Jack. Make a new plan, Stan. ... Just drop off the key, Lee, and get yourself free."

As I sit here writing this chapter, I still cannot quite believe that I had the gall to just quit a job. I had no intention of quitting that day, I promise. But I had had enough, and it was time to go. I did not have a lot of money to sustain myself, and had not thought of leaving, or at least not on that day. I had some savings, but not enough to justify taking the walk.

I wonder how many of you have thought about saying to a boss: "I quit. You can have this job. I cannot take this stress any longer. I am out of here Missy Boss Lady or Boss Man. Color me gone."

I felt as though I had a true out-of-body experience. I am a professional. What would move someone like me to just say those words, "I quit" and mean it? Two months later, I still cannot believe that I quit. Please allow me the privilege of giving you a brief recap of what happened that day.

The night before, at a networking event, I learned that my partner, the Golden Child, was giving her resignation to the boss that next day. I felt sad, and I had been through another sleepless night. I felt helpless as I watched an excellent employee leaving the firm due to unprofessional management.

Not long before that, one of the owners of the company had approached me for a conversation. Evidently co-workers in other departments had tipped him off that my partner and I were not happy with our boss's management style. The big-wig and I talked, and I could tell he did not want to get involved. He seemed shocked by a couple of things I related to him about my boss. But he hid most of his actual feelings well.

The big-wig expressed firmly that he did not want my partner or me to leave the company. He knew the Golden Child and I had just both won a nation-wide contest. He said he valued our contributions to the growth of the new legal division.

His advice was to talk to my boss, something I had already done many times. When the conversation ended, I was thinking "Why did you press me to call you in private if you did not really want the truth about what goes on in our office?" I decided I would not call him again on that subject. He would have to instigate any future meeting.

Even though I did not think it would be fruitful, I did as the big-wig asked. I approached my boss and told her how her fighting with the Golden Child was very upsetting and distracting to me. I asked that she ease up on my co-worker, let her do her work. I said the Golden Child had been with the company eight months and was doing a great job. She did not need to be micro-managed.

The Golden Child and I had become a great team, and we were finally making progress in our tough market. I could not tell my boss that I knew the Golden Child was going to resign, and I could tell that the boss was not interested in doing anything differently. I also knew that, with the Golden Child gone, my clients would have to work with my boss. I knew that would not work well, so I felt doomed.

Our boss was very pushy and unconcerned about our clients' needs. We had tried to break down for her the ways in which our market did not welcome change. She just did not get it. Well, she did not get much of anything about how we worked, yet we were succeeding in our tough market.

As I worked to build client relationships and to maintain some with clients I had worked with for years, our boss would tear down the relationships. She would ask for my thoughts and then ignore them. She was not very tuned in to other people. Not what you'd call a jewel of a boss.

I am writing this on the eve of three months since I walked away from that firm. I am not presently working. I am taking my time looking, hoping to get the right working environment for me this time.

I must admit that, with pressing financial obligations, I often ask myself if I could have stayed longer. Should I have stayed? Every time I get the same answer: I was in a very toxic environment. I HAD TO LEAVE.

Each of us sometimes has to ask ourself whether it's worth the money to stay in a toxic job. Is it worth poor health? It is worth the sadness that comes from working in a toxic environment?

Think about it. What if someone told you that you would die if you did not move out of your lovely house that is very toxic to your health? I think you and I both agree we would run fast from a situation like that. Staying would not be worth the damages that could take place. We can find another house, just as we can get another job.

Too many people today allow their income to define them as a person. I believe that our caliber, our beliefs and our morals are what truly define each of us as a person, not our position or money. Health is wealth. Please remember this when you decide to stay with a boss from hell.

Chapter 10
How to Overcome
the Lasting Effects of the
Boss From Hell

As I sit here on my lonely, very lonely and very broke days, I have had much time to reflect on this matter. I decided to just get over it.

You know life comes at you fast. Each of us will experience many things during our life-span – some good, and some bad. One of the things I am most proud of is the wisdom to forgive and forget the passing pain and challenges that life can bring, and the ability to press on in a positive state of mind.

I am happy that I know how to reflect on what has happened to me, learn from it, and move on. I will freely admit that sometimes this is not instant. It may take me a while to do so.

But I believe I am able to dissect my behavior and my actions, to see what I could have done differently. I am able to forgive others and myself, and to truly get on with my life and my business.

I feel strongly that arrogance looks like arrogance, but it may be translated into fear or pain. I believe that, if we could closely examine the past lives or the childhood of a boss from hell, we would uncover some deep and sad emotions. These people do not feel as good or as confident about themselves as they would have us think. It has been easier for me to pray and forgive these bosses because of these insights.

Think about it! If you really are happy and in charge of your own life, would you not portray this in your everyday life and in the world around you? Would not a happy person transform into a happier boss, wife, husband, and good human being, period? Would not the joy of this person feeling like he or she has truly made it be contagious?

I know you said, "yes!" And I agree. People who act and think like hell feel like hell inside. Now, I am no psychology major, but I do have a lot of common sense. And I am a life-long studier of people, paying attention to them because I like people.

At times we get confused when we think about the American Dream. If we look good, smell good and we have MONEY, we are pronounced level-headed and happy. Add education, and we have got it going on! Sometimes, though, this could not be farther from the truth.

I have seen people of many cultures, education, and economic backgrounds who have added significantly to this world we live in, in huge and positive ways.

So, when we think about these past or present bosses from hell, let's have a little sympathy. You don't have to keep working for them. Let's be sure to remember they are the ones with the problems. Please wish them well and get on with your life.

There is something good out here waiting just for you. Keep moving!

Chapter 11
Let's Move On

I am going to make this short and sweet. There is no need to carry this on and on. We simply need to move on.

"Let's move on" is easier said than done. Any of us can analyze over and over again, and back and forth about the circumstance involving a boss from hell. Yes, you can rethink the situation until you are blue in the face. But one thing we must all agree with is that you cannot move on until you let go.

So, let's all take a deep breath and let go of the pain inside, let go of the broken self-pride.

Let go and let God direct our steps to a better place that will not duplicate what we have just experienced.

What was is gone forever. It is all in the past. We must learn to forgive ourselves for being in a dysfunctional relationship with our present or former company, and move on. The lesson we have just learned could be a large factor in moving to our next level of success.

Again, I say: THERE IS SOMETHING GOOD OUT THERE, WAITING FOR YOU!

DISCLAIMER
Evil/Mean Personal Disclaimer

I am not a mean or evil person. I do not enjoy talking about people in an unkind manner. I believe a person is innocent until proven guilty.

I look for the good in people first. But I cannot stay blind to bad.

When I was a child, my mother always said, "If you do not have anything good to say about a person, don't say anything at all." This is a philosophy I have aspired to live by most of my life. My mom was a good lady. She taught me some valuable things.

However, I have found in my journey through life that sometimes you have to speak out and call it like it is. As others would put it, "keep it real." I totally agree with this saying, and especially when there is even a remote possibility that I could help or encourage someone. Or even let them know that I somewhat understand. This is what I am about, assisting others and speaking the truth.

There is a saying that "the truth hurts." This can be true, but sometimes the truth helps, and it could set you free. And maybe it helps us – if only to reflect or think about our actions.

I was the child who was always asking my mom and others, "Is this fair?" Or stating "That's just not fair or kind or whatever."

My inspiration to write this book is linked to those same questions and feelings that are deeply rooted inside me. I have always had a strong passion for people and fairness, and nothing has changed in that regard.

Thank you for purchasing and reading my book. I pray that this information is helpful to you or someone you care about.

Gale Jackson

February 2017

About the Author

Gale Jackson is a champion of fair treatment of people, diversity inclusion, and peace, and has been since childhood. She is a born leader who grew up in Chicago in an escalated domestic violence home. Gale learned early in life that she was gifted in the areas of conflict resolution and negotiation. She has worked in several states as a successful paralegal and human resources recruiter, consulting with prestigious law firms and corporations.

Gale is a powerful advocate and frequently-requested keynote speaker. She speaks out strongly against domestic violence and the hostile work environment, and about the effects those issues have on individuals, families, and our society. Her goal is to change those vicious cycles through education, empowerment and encouragement.

Gale has a bubbly, fun-loving personality. She is creative, honest, confident, humble, and warm-hearted, and she has a strong passion for people.

www.ingramcontent.com/pod-product-compliance
Lightning Source LLC
Chambersburg PA
CBHW060100050426
42448CB00011B/2549